Careers For
Number
Lovers

Interviews by Andrew Kaplan

Photographs by Eddie Keating and Carrie Boretz

CHOICES
The Millbrook Press
Brookfield, Connecticut

Produced in association with Agincourt Press.

Photographs by Eddie Keating, except: Ruri Yampolsky (Jim Berry),
Eugene Fasullo (Carrie Boretz), John Scott (Carrie Boretz), Paul
Hodge (Natalie Stultz), Lois Grippo (Carrie Boretz), Joel
Schneider (Carrie Boretz), Don Crocket (Craig Sailor).

Cataloging-in-Publication Data

Kaplan, Andrew.
Careers for number lovers/interviews by Andrew Kaplan,
photographs by Eddie Keating and Carrie Boretz.

64 p.; ill.: (Choices)
Bibliography: p.
Includes index.

Summary: Interviews with fourteen people who work in careers of
interest to young people who like mathematics.
1. Mathematics – Vocational guidance. (Mathematics – Study and teaching).
I. Keating, Eddie, ill.   II. Boretz, Carrie, ill.
III. Title.   IV. Series.
QA 10.5 K141   1991   510.23 KAP
ISBN 1-878841-47-5
ISBN 0-87884-147-5 (pbk.)

123456789 - WO - 96 95 94 93 92

Contents

Introduction

In this book, 14 people who work in math-related fields talk about their careers — what their work involves, how they got started, and what they like (and dislike) about it. They tell you things you should know before beginning a math-related career and show you how feeling comfortable with numbers can lead to many different types of jobs.

Many math-related jobs are found in the sciences, such as physics and seismology, and the applied sciences, such as engineering. But just as many others use math much less formally. Pollsters and actuaries, for instance, use math to interpret population data, while casino managers use it to monitor casino profits and navigators use it to sail safely from one port to another. You don't have to know any advanced math to be a statistician, but you do have to do a lot of figuring.

The 14 careers described here are just the beginning, so don't limit your sights. At the end of this book, you'll find short descriptions of a dozen more careers you may want to explore, as well as suggestions on how to get more information. Math is everywhere in the business world. If you're a number lover, you'll find a wide range of career choices open to you.

Joan B. Storey, M.B.A., M.S.W.
Series Career Consultant

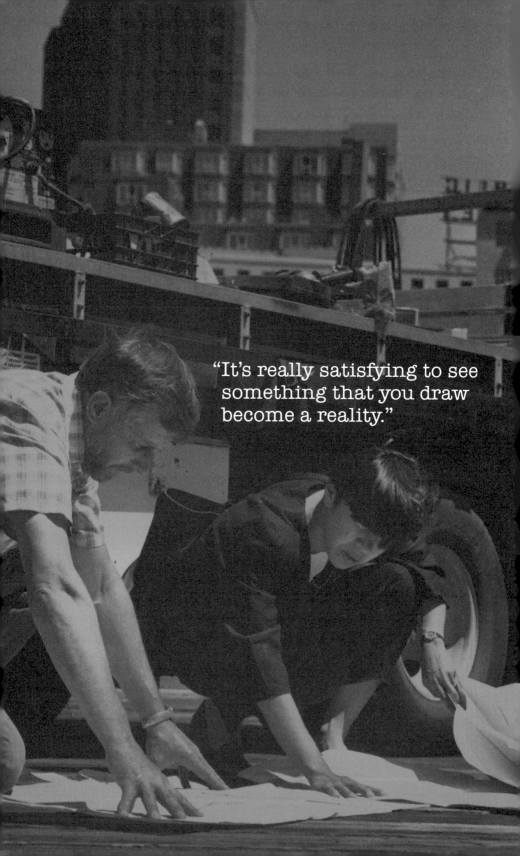

"It's really satisfying to see something that you draw become a reality."

RURI YAMPOLSKY

ARCHITECT

Seattle, Washington

WHAT I DO:
For the most part, I design and plan home renovations, but I've also done some office and commercial work.

Generally, there's a set procedure for renovation work. First, we go in and measure the space, locating all the plumbing and electrical fixtures. If the building is old, we ask a structural engineer to determine whether the structure is still sound. After our inspection, we use all this information to draw up a floor plan.

On a second plan, we show all the changes that must be made to adapt the space to our client's needs. The client gives input, and then we revise. Finally, we draw up construction docu-

Ruri and a co-worker look over blueprints at a site. Blueprints use exact measurements to show how something should be built.

ments with exact measurements that show specifically how something is to be built.

On the surface, architecture doesn't seem very related to math. But numbers are everywhere. To make and use plans, for instance, you have to be comfortable with measurements, ratios, and figures drawn to scale.

Other calculations also come up regularly, such as calculating the loads, or forces, bearing on particular beams or walls. When you study structures, as you must in order to get your architecture license, you learn how to calculate these loads. The math here is very important, because you have to know the load in order to choose the best material for the job. A wooden beam, for instance, might break under a load that a steel beam could carry. If you make a mistake in your calculations, the whole house can fall down.

HOW I GOT STARTED:

I became interested in architecture when I was about 12 years old. I liked to draw rooms and make models of houses. It wasn't too much later that I realized I would be an architect.

While I was in school, I had various jobs related to architecture. In college, I worked at the architecture library. And between my first and second years at graduate school in architecture, I worked for a firm that did drawings of rental properties. After that, I did work for a large architectural office.

HOW I FEEL ABOUT IT:

I like my work. It's creative, and it's really satisfying to see something that you draw become a reality. But sometimes people have unreasonable expectations. Either they want something done for an impossibly low cost, or they're asking for something that just can't be fit into the space that's available. In these cases, you have to be diplomatic and help people see that what they want just can't be done. Then you find an alternative. If they respond well, it's quite satisfying.

WHAT YOU SHOULD KNOW:

Students who think they might want to be architects should get part-time or summer work in an architecture office. You run errands, help

As an architect, Ruri needs good drafting skills.

Ruri describes work that will be done at a site.

the architects, and get a feel for the profession.

Generally, the requirements for an architecture license are a professional degree and three years' experience in an office. Then you take a four-day qualifying exam, which tests your knowledge of everything from structure to the history of architecture. In one part of the exam you have to design a building from start to finish in 12 hours.

There are a lot of different skills involved in architecture, so offices look for people with different strengths. For example, I'm not the fastest draftsperson, but I have good managerial and math skills. Other people are better at designing or overseeing construction, and still others specialize in CAD, which is computer-aided design.

You have to have a strong interest in architecture to like this work because the hours are long, over 40 per week. In fact, the pay is not very high when you consider the amount of education involved. A starting architect in a big firm may make $20,000. An architect with five years' experience makes about $40,000. Naturally, there's a lot of money at the top, but that's just for a very small group of people.

"This work is for people who can imagine solutions and then put them into practice."

EUGENE FASULLO

STRUCTURAL ENGINEER

New York, New York

WHAT I DO:
I'm deputy director of engineering and deputy chief engineer for the Port Authority of New York and New Jersey. I'm responsible for the daily operation of a 1200-person engineering department that's involved with the design, construction, operation, and rebuilding of all kinds of public facilities — airports, tunnels, bridges, bus terminals, a heliport, and so on.

My staff and I figure out the engineering concepts involved in a project and then determine how best to apply them. Often, this process starts with my original field, structural engineering. Using the principles of structural engineering, we can create

Structural engineers like Eugene use mathematical models to design such public works as bridges, tunnels, and airports.

mathematical models from which predictions can be made. For example, we use models to calculate the impact of gravity on a building or the effect of an earthquake on a bridge. Then we apply what we learn to the design of the structure. Mathematical models tell us how big and how strong each part has to be.

One example of the kind of problem I've worked on is the building I'm sitting in — the World Trade Center. A building of this height — 110 stories — is subject to tremendous wind forces. To find out what they would be like, we made computer models and did wind tunnel tests that predicted and simulated how the building would sway. Then we put people into rooms that swayed in a similar way so that we could tell whether or not these kinds of movements ruled out human occupancy.

11

Eugene works in his office in the World Trade Center.

HOW I GOT STARTED:

I've always been interested in construction. When I was a kid, my hobbies were woodworking and furniture building. This evolved into an interest in architecture, which I studied at Brooklyn Technical High School. Then, after a stint in the military, I got a B.A. in civil engineering and a master's in structural engineering. I chose this field because of its relation to construction and because it would enable me to work on useful projects — bridges, tunnels, and so on — that would contribute to society.

After graduate school, I started working for the Port Authority. I began as a trainee and rotated through different assignments. These included work on the George Washington Bridge and in the design department. Then I worked my way up the line.

HOW I FEEL ABOUT IT:

The most important thing to me is the idea that I'm making a difference in people's experience of life. I like contributing to society and doing something that is worthwhile. That's what professionalism is all about. My definition of "profession" is a vocation in which what you practice is not just for personal gain but for the good of people in general.

Public sector work has one frustrating element, though. Sometimes, a project's size, scale, and final design get influenced by issues that are not strictly related to engineering but instead are more related to business, politics, and finance. So, while you may have a wonderful scheme that will serve humankind, other considerations may keep it from being built or from being done the way you have envisioned it.

WHAT YOU SHOULD KNOW: This work is for people who can imagine solutions and then put them into practice. What's important are desire, creativity, and commitment. You need the willingness to imagine what is possible and then to go out and do it.

Pay and hours reflect the fact that engineers are professionals. Port Authority engineers start at about $30,000 per year, and our chief makes about $150,000. The hours, for someone who is committed, go beyond nine-to-five. I attend conferences, read journals, and have taken and taught classes. It's a case of ongoing education, which is a positive experience — one that keeps you in touch with new ideas and people. This is just one more advantage of the work.

Eugene looks over signs announcing renovation plans.

"Of course, above all, I love the sea."

JOHN SCOTT

NAVIGATOR

New York, New York

WHAT I DO:
I'm the first officer aboard the *Cunard Countess,* which is a cruise ship that travels between Puerto Rico and other islands in the Caribbean. My primary responsibility is navigating the ship for eight hours each day.

I go to sea for eight weeks at a time. Then I have eight weeks off. When I'm sailing, I have the same basic schedule. I get up at 3:40 every morning so that I can take over the ship at 4:00 A.M. From then until we dock at 8:00 A.M., I navigate the approach to the harbor we're visiting that day. Later, at 4:00 P.M., I guide the ship out of the harbor and navigate it until 8:00 P.M.

All of navigation is basically mathematics. Some calculations are simple, such as working out our arrival time, the distance between two places, or the ship's speed. But others are more complicated. For instance, we use computers to chart courses and monitor ship stability, to help keep the ship upright. But even with computers, you need a feeling for the math so that you can double-check what's going on. You need to understand the principles.

When we're on the open sea, for example, we have to calculate our position using signals from satellites because there are no landmarks in sight. Computers interpret those signals for us. But I also use a sextant and star charts, just as the old-time sailors did, so that I can double-check the position myself.

John guides the path of the *Cunard Countess* from the bridge of the luxury liner.

HOW I GOT STARTED:
I grew up in New Zealand, and when I was 10 years old,

I decided I would go to sea. After I graduated from high school, I served a four-year apprenticeship as a trainee navigator, learning the job from the bottom up. I did everything from chipping rust off the ship's bottom to learning about ship construction and meteorology, which is the study of weather. You have to know all of this — the basics of running a ship — if you want to pilot one.

When I finished the apprenticeship, I got my first certificate of competency, which is a second officer's certificate. Then I did two more years at sea, and got my chief officer's certificate. Finally, I spent another 18 months at sea and got my master's, or captain's, certificate.

HOW I FEEL ABOUT IT:
I love my work and enjoy the challenge and responsibility of guiding a large ship. The travel is another bonus — I've been around the world six times. And of course, above all, I love the sea. It has a certain beauty, and it never fails to fascinate me when I watch it each morning.

Besides waking up at 3:40 in the morning, there's nothing that I don't like about the job. The only real problem I encounter is that shoreside people don't understand what I do. I'm away for a period of

John finds some time to relax with a co-worker.

Navigators today still use star charts and sextants.

time, but when I'm back home I'm not working. So no one really believes that I do any work.

WHAT YOU SHOULD KNOW: If you're interested in a career at sea, you should follow these steps: At school, concentrate on science and especially math if you want to navigate. Then, after high school, apply to a maritime academy. Once you've trained there and become qualified, you can go to sea. The training process is similar to the one I've been through. You work your way up, gaining different levels of certification.

Besides a love of the sea, you also need certain character traits to survive on a ship.

You need a calm temperament, and you've got to have some courage because you're going to be in charge of a ship at a very young age. You've got to take responsibility and be confident that you're making the right decisions. You've also got to be able to get along with people because you're living in a small community – a ship is really like a self-contained town.

There is a good future in this work. The industry is expanding, so there's a demand for skilled navigators, and this demand is improving salaries. Although pay depends on a ship's size and prestige, it can be quite good. On an American ship, a master can make over $100,000 a year.

"I've been part of the opening-up of the entire outer solar system."

LANNY MILLER

PHYSICIST

Pasadena, California

WHAT I DO:
I work for the Jet Propulsion Laboratory on the Voyager project, which launches unmanned space probes. I've been with the laboratory for 17 years now, and I've had a number of different positions. At the beginning, my work was primarily technical — involving physics, engineering, and computer work. Later, my responsibilities included more managerial functions.

My first job on Voyager involved navigation and maneuvers. There are two components to navigation. The first is finding out where you are in relation to where you want to be. The second is planning a course correction to get from the one to the other. With Voyager, we knew we were starting from the

Earth, and we also knew we wanted Voyager to fly by as many of the other planets in the solar system as possible. The problem was that the planets are always moving in their orbits around the sun. So we had to chart a course that took the orbits into account.

Before the spacecraft was launched, we made a model of the solar system and tested various courses. We had to calculate the best time to launch, the maneuvers that would have to be made, and how much fuel would be required to make them. This kind of modeling is called Monte Carlo analysis, and I formulated the equations that were necessary for it. Although I did most of the technical work myself, I also had computer programmers who helped me.

As the years went on, I did other projects at JPL, but eventually I came back to

Lanny uses both math and physics to plot the course a space probe will take.

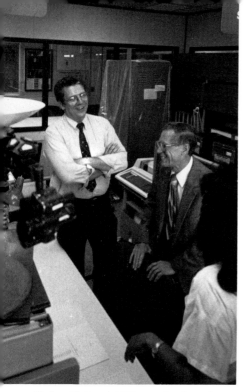

Scientists at JPL work closely together on project teams.

Voyager as manager of the flight engineering office. As we prepared for Voyager's fly-by of Neptune, I spent three years supervising three teams of engineers: the spacecraft team, which monitored and maintained the spacecraft and its systems; the navigation team, which charted and corrected Voyager's course; and the sequence team, which put together the series of commands that would tell the spacecraft what we wanted it to do.

HOW I GOT STARTED:
I got interested in science in high school when I took a biology course. After that, I took a physics course and got even more interested. I decided that I wanted to get into physics, and that's exactly what I did, never deviating. In college, I took a double major in math and physics, and later got a doctorate in physics.

My original plan was to teach at a university. However, at that time, in 1968, the schools were flooded with physics and math professors. So I looked around for other things to do. One opportunity that came my way was working on the Apollo manned space program in Houston. Since the moon shots intrigued me, I took the job.

I worked in Houston for five years before moving on to JPL. While I was in Houston, I applied physics to a number of technical problems involved in the Apollo and Skylab programs. For instance, one of my projects involved helping astronauts learn to use shadows on the moon to navigate, in case they ever lost use of their computers.

HOW I FEEL ABOUT IT:
It's been exciting. In a sense, I've been part of the opening-up of the entire outer solar system. Voyager gave us the first close-up pictures of Neptune. It's also the first

spacecraft to have sent back detailed descriptive information about the three largest outer planets: Jupiter, Saturn, and Uranus.

WHAT YOU SHOULD KNOW: The space program involves people from lots of different backrounds. Obviously, some of those people are trained in astronomy and planetary science. But we also hire many different types of engineers, and people involved with computer science. In all of these disciplines, though, strong math skills are a prerequisite. In fact, there's a lot of statistical analysis in this field, and sometimes we hire straight mathematicians.

The pay in this work is good. Entry-level engineering and scientific jobs at JPL are competitive with those in private industry. But I want to emphasize that the rewards of space exploration go way beyond the financial ones. We enjoy what we're doing, and we feel it's valuable not only for the country, but for humankind as well.

Lanny explains how a satellite works to two students.

"If an earthquake comes,
your social plans go out
the window."

KATE HUTTON

SEISMOLOGIST

Pasadena, California

WHAT I DO:
I supervise data processing for the California Seismic Network, which is a service that gathers and analyzes data on earthquake activity. Because earthquakes are so common in Southern California, where we're located, and because they can do so much damage, it's important for us to know as much as possible about them. The better we understand earthquakes, the more accurately we can predict when they're going to occur and how strong they'll be.

My job includes many different functions, most of them technical. The first thing I do each morning is make sure all the equipment in our 250 different instrument stations is running properly. Because all the

Earthquake activity is usually measured on machines called seismographs.

equipment is networked, I can run all the tests I need to from the main office terminal. When the stations are working properly, they feed seismic data from all over Southern California into our headquarters at the California Institute of Technology in Pasadena.

When it's quiet, the hours are generally nine to five, but sometimes an alarm goes off at 3:00 A.M. and people are called in to see what's going on. If there's a lot of seismic activity, this can happen four or five nights in a row. Usually, though, it only happens about twice each month.

When the alarm does go off, we follow the same basic procedure that we do at any other time: we locate the earthquake and assign a magnitude to it. The magnitude depends on the duration and the strength of the heaves. It's measured on the Richter scale, which is a logarithmic

Kate examines a printout from one of the seismographs.

scale. An earthquake measuring 6.0 on the Richter scale, for instance, is 10 times more powerful than an earthquake measuring 5.0.

Machines do much of the data processing, but we interpret the results and explain them to the public. To do this, an understanding of the math and physics involved is crucial. Without an understanding of the underlying principles, the numbers would just be chatter.

HOW I GOT STARTED:
Originally, I was interested in astronomy, and that was what I studied in college and graduate school. But after I got my Ph.D., I found that there weren't many jobs in

astronomy, so I got work in seismology.

The fact that my degrees are in astronomy is a bit unusual for this field. In a certain way, however, it makes a lot of sense. Both astronomy and seismology, which is a branch of geophysics, are applications of the same basic scientific principles. To be an astronomer, you need to understand physics, math, and computers. To be a geophysicist or a seismologist, you need to understand those same things.

HOW I FEEL ABOUT IT:
This job is unpredictable, which is both good and bad. The variety is great — you never know what's coming.

The earthquakes can be small or large, and you don't know whether people will feel them or not. Of course, this unpredictability is also a problem. If an earthquake comes, your social plans go out the window.

WHAT YOU SHOULD KNOW: If you're interested in getting into this field, you should study physics, geology, computer science, and math. I want to emphasize that it's important to study as much math and physics as you can, as early as you can, because math is the basis of almost everything we do. Data comes in numerical form, and if you want to use it, you've got to know how to work with the numbers. If you don't like math, you won't do well in geophysics because there's too much of it involved with the work.

Another application of seismology is oil exploration. Geophysicists set off small explosions and study the seismic waves they produce in order to determine the structure of the earth in a particular area. This helps them locate the most likely places to drill.

In fact, the demand for geophysicists, seismologists included, varies with the price of oil. When the price of oil is high, oil companies hire more geophysicists to help them find untapped reserves. This in turn drives up salaries. In a university setting such as mine, though, you almost always make less money than you would working for an oil company. But in the right job, it's still possible to make a good living.

Seismologists must have some background in computers.

"It's a lot harder to mark a line on a hillside than to mark that line on a map."

PAUL HODGE

SURVEYOR

Montpelier, Vermont

WHAT I DO:

I'm the chief of surveying for the Vermont Agency of Transportation. Basically, what we do is go out to an area and map it. We fill about 100 survey requests a year. Some of the more common requests are for bridge and road relocations, but we do right-of-way surveys and jurisdictional surveys, too.

In a typical bridge survey, we lay a line 400 feet before and after the bridge site. The line is the path that the approaches to the bridge will take. Planners can draw a line on a map, but it's a lot harder to mark a line on a hillside than it is to mark that line on a map.

After we lay the line, we make a map of the site. We show the new bridge location, and we also provide 15-

foot sectional profiles of the terrain. That is, we divide the total length of the bridge and its approaches into 15-foot sections, and describe each of those sections in detail. Engineers then use these profiles to design the bridge.

In road relocations, the county or state wants an existing road moved. For example, a really tight curve might have to be straightened out. In that case, we survey the existing curve and make a map. Then we find a better line for the curve and survey the new line. Sometimes this leads to right-of-way surveys, which determine where state property ends and private property begins.

The last kind of survey is the jurisdictional survey, which involves identifying town and county lines. In murder cases, for example, somebody must go into court and say for sure that the body was found within a certain

27

It's difficult to mark a line on hilly terrain. Paul oversees the mapping for this area.

HOW I GOT STARTED:

Originally, I wanted to go to forestry school. That was at the time of the Vietnam War, though, and I went into the service instead. I took up construction surveying when I was stationed in Thailand.

When I got out of the service, I worked for an engineer. We worked on interstate highways, property surveys, and urban renewal projects. Then I went to Vermont Technical College, where I got a two-year associate's degree in surveying. After that, I worked at a large firm for two years and got my license.

town's lines and that therefore that town's police force has jurisdiction. That's my responsibility, and I represent both the agency and the state.

There's a lot of math involved in surveying. Much of it involves measurements. When you're laying lines, you're always calculating the angles and distances of curves and slopes. There's also lots of work with map coordinates and elevations, or heights. You need a strong background in trigonometry and geometry, which you get when you study civil engineering.

HOW I FEEL ABOUT IT:

My work is very interesting because I get paid for putting puzzles together. When I do historical work with county lines or rights-of-way, I'm like a detective. I get all of the existing surveys together, some of which date back as much as 200 years. Then I use a computer to lay one survey on top of another. This way I can see how the lines and the roads have shifted over the years.

WHAT YOU SHOULD KNOW:

The fastest way to get into this field is to get a two-year associate's degree in civil engineering, but you'll be better off in the end if you get a four-year B.A. or even a master's degree. If you don't want a degree, you can apprentice yourself to a surveyor. But that takes many years, and you'll be missing out on some important background.

To make it through your engineering studies and the job, you have to be comfortable with math, especially geometry and trigonometry. Also, along with satellite technology and aerial photography, computers are becoming increasingly important as surveying responds to the new technologies now available.

In my department, the pay ranges from $7.00 to $14.00 an hour, depending on your education and experience. Like any job, though, there are regional variations in pay. Places like New York and California pay more because it costs more to live there. Also, surveyors who work for private companies make more money.

The end results of Paul's surveys are 15-foot sectional profiles.

"This is a business of pennies, and you have to be exacting to survive."

KEVIN CANADA

PRODUCT MANAGER

Randolph, New Jersey

WHAT I DO:
I do marketing for a major food corporation, which means that I design sales strategies. Right now, I'm working with the project manager of a margarine brand. We're responsible for its profit and loss. Our job is to make the product as profitable as possible.

There are a number of ways we can work to achieve higher profits. One way entails working with the sales force, trying to increase the sales volume. This usually increases profits, too. But building volume also involves spending money on sales promotions and the like, so we have to be careful that we're not spending more on the promotion than we're making on the increased sales.

Kevin discusses marketing strategies and price structures with co-workers.

Another way to increase profits is through changes in our pricing policy. Prices are all interrelated mathematically. A larger size package should always cost less per ounce than a smaller size package. To keep all the prices rational, we calculate them using a mathematical tool called a matrix, which relates numbers to one another. A magic square in which the columns and rows all add up to the same number is a simple example of a matrix.

Changing prices will change a product's market share because people will generally buy more of a less expensive product and less of a more expensive one. But just as with sales promotions, we have to be careful that we're not losing more money on the changes than what we're taking in because of the increased volume. To figure this out, we use mathematical formulas to simulate what will happen given a certain price change. No mathematical model is perfect, of course, but the better your understanding of math, the better your predictions will be.

All of this involves lots of data, detail, and painstaking analysis. But this is a tough business, a business of pennies, and you have to be exacting to survive.

HOW I GOT STARTED:
My interest in business started in college. Until that point, I didn't have any corporate aspirations. In fact,

when I was in high school, I was thinking about becoming a firefighter. But then I got involved in athletics, and that led me to college on a scholarship, and college led me into business.

After college, I got an M.B.A., a master's degree in business administration. In both college and graduate school, mathematics played a big role in my studies. As an undergraduate, I took straight math courses such as calculus and statistics. In business school, I took classes in data analysis and other math-related fields such as accounting and economics.

Demographics are important in Kevin's job.

If there's a problem with this job, it's that you do a lot of things over and over again. As circumstances change, or management opinions change, I'm called on to revise plans that I've already made. Occasionally I've had to change things up to seven times. It's part of the job, but the repetition is frustrating — especially when, after all the changes, the final plan is the same as the one I originally came up with.

Kevin looks over some new data. He uses mathematical models to set pricing policy for the products he manages.

HOW I FEEL ABOUT IT:

What I like best about the job is the high degree of autonomy, or freedom, that I have. I'm given a responsibility and a deadline for carrying it out, but nothing more. I'm not given any structure beyond that, so I'm able to handle things in my own way, the way that seems most efficient to me.

WHAT YOU SHOULD KNOW:

The career path in this field is pretty straightforward. You need an M.B.A. Some people work their way into marketing without one, but eventually many companies require them to get the degree as part of their advancement.

To work in marketing, you have to be good at quantitative analysis. You also have to write and speak well so that you can convey to other people your understanding of what the data means.

The pay in this work is good, but you definitely work hard for it. I'm here an average of 55 or 60 hours each week, and there have been weeks when the total has been much greater. So while I'm paid well, I'm not certain I'd like to work it out on an hourly basis.

"Ever since I was a kid, I've been interested in sports, especially sports statistics."

JIM SAMIA

STATISTICIAN

Boston, Massachusetts

WHAT I DO:
I'm the director of statistics for the Boston Red Sox. My main responsibilities are calculating players' statistics and providing these statistics to the Red Sox management and the press. Also, because I'm part of the public relations department, I check press credentials and arrange player interviews and autograph sessions.

My responsibilities vary during the year. During the season, I keep a "day-by-day" book in which I record what each player does in every game. From that book, I calculate trends, tables, and the statistics that I enter into my computer.

Some statistics are for the public and the press. For example, before each game I write the press notes, which

list interesting bits of information that a broadcaster might want to mention between batters. When you hear "Reed is batting .298 with runners on base," that bit of information comes from the press notes.

I also come up with numbers that are solely for the Red Sox management. These statistics describe each player's performance in specific situations, such as his batting average against right-handed pitchers at night, or other players' performances against the Red Sox. Often the manager will come to me with a request for a specific statistic, and then I'll calculate it.

The hours depend on the season. In the off-season, from October to February, mine is a nine-to-five job. During spring training, when I'm with the team in Florida, I get to the ballpark at eight and work until the

Jim uses a scorecard to keep an accurate statistical record of each day's game.

35

end of that day's game, which is usually around six.

During the season, though, the hours are long. When the team is at home, I start at nine in the morning and work until two hours after the game ends, which is usually after midnight for a night game. I also travel with the team for about 70 percent of the road schedule. When I'm on the road, I'm really working all the time.

HOW I GOT STARTED:
Ever since I was young, I've been interested in sports, especially statistics. Being good at math, I found that I had a knack for keeping them.

My interest in sports eventually led me to a college major in sports management. The program I was in covered both the business and administrative aspects of sports. I took classes in sports law and sports marketing, as well as more basic business courses like accounting. I used the program to work toward a job in professional sports. Other people who study sports management work in college sports or do things like managing health clubs.

HOW I FEEL ABOUT IT:
I'm working at something that I like to do. It is work —

Jim observes the game from his perch in the press box.

A computer helps Jim calculate statistics quickly.

there are long hours, particularly during the season — but it's something that I enjoy doing, so the time passes easily. Also, I like baseball, and this job keeps me involved with the sport. I like being around the players and watching the games.

Like any job, though, this one has its difficulties. I have to deal with a lot of different people — players, the press, the fans — and some of them can be difficult. But it's all part of my job; if a player has had a tough day and is in a bad mood, I have to be sensitive to that.

WHAT YOU SHOULD KNOW:
The job requires a college education. While there's no specific major you should

take — you don't absolutely need a degree in sports management — you should have a strong background in communications as well as math. Everything our office does, from providing statistics to responding to fans' complaints, involves communications. So it's necessary to study something that's related — like journalism, public relations, or communications broadcasting.

The pay is decent, but a little bit on the low end when you compare it to similar jobs in other businesses. I make less than an accountant with five years' experience. But I can't complain — the job pays the bills, and I like what I'm doing.

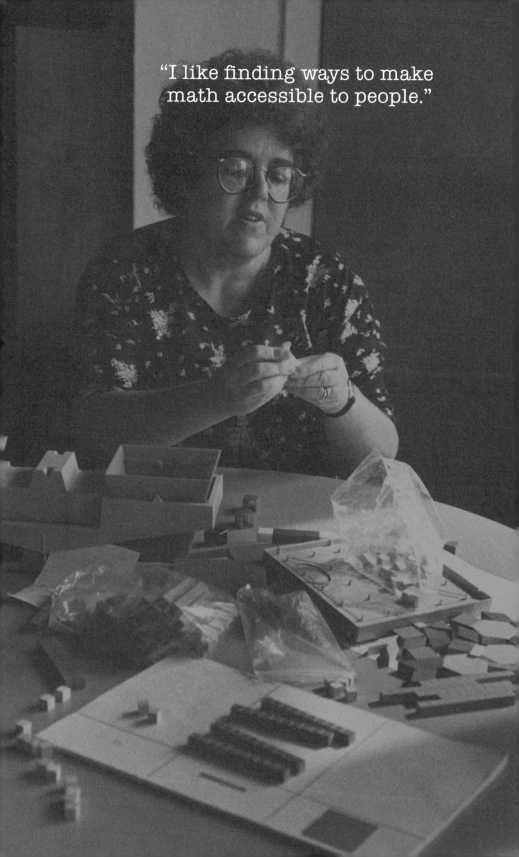

"I like finding ways to make math accessible to people."

LOIS GRIPPO
MATH TEXTBOOK EDITOR

New York, New York

WHAT I DO:

I work for a company that is hired by various large publishers to write and design textbooks. We work with these companies to develop series of books that will be sold to schools all over the country. Most often, we are asked to work on series that include books for kindergarten through eighth grade. But even though we're involved in every phase of the books' development, you don't see our name on the finished books. Only the publisher's name appears.

Right now, I'm senior supervisor of mathematics for kindergarten through fifth grade. I'm in touch with the series authors, who are all experts in math education. But the authors don't usually write the books. In-

stead, they determine what the books' educational philosophy should be. For instance, authors decide how much geometry to include and how much review material there should be.

After getting the authors' input, my company and the client develop the structure of the books. We create sample lessons and a table of contents for each book in the series. The sample stage can be long, because a lot of people are involved – authors, the client, math teachers, the owners of my company – and we have to revise the samples to reflect everyone's comments. When we finally finish, we test our sample lessons on teachers and students.

After the samples are set, we write and edit the books. I explain to writers and editors how to create a lesson -- what the structure should be, and what it should look

The editors meet to look over new material.

like. Then I read what's produced, and make sure that it's consistent with the series philosophy. I also make sure that the lesson sequence makes sense — that nothing is being taught out of sequence or before all the building blocks for a particular skill have been introduced.

HOW I GOT STARTED:

I began as a copyeditor for a major publishing house. At one point, the only project available was in math, checking answers. I had never liked math before, but I thought it would be easy to work as an answer checker. After all, it was only elementary school math.

I was wrong about the job being easy. There were lots of concepts I hadn't learned before. But soon I found that I loved math. I realized that if I had had the right teacher when I was a kid, I would have liked math all along. I decided that I wanted to help make that difference for kids. I wanted to help them learn and like math when they were young, instead of when they were adults. That desire led me into math writing and eventually into the position I have now.

HOW I FEEL ABOUT IT:
The most interesting part of this work is figuring out how to help people get past the problems they have with math. I like finding ways to make math accessible to people.

Companies like mine, though, have the same problems and pressures as major publishing houses, plus a few of their own. There's schedule pressure, which is common throughout publishing.

WHAT YOU SHOULD KNOW:
In this field, you have to be comfortable with math. In fact, you have to like it. That doesn't mean you have to be an expert. We almost never do books above the eighth-grade level, so you don't have to know calculus or other high-level topics. But you do have to have a feel for the subject. It's very hard to teach someone about numbers if you don't have a good sense of them yourself.

The hours and the pay vary. When you've got a deadline to meet, you can be working 60-hour weeks. Between projects, though, when you're looking for work, the hours are light. As for the pay, you won't get rich, but you can make a decent living. An editor with five years of experience can make $35,000 to $40,000. Supervisors and project heads make more.

Hours are long when there's a deadline to meet.

"I know how to focus on a body of data and find the hidden relationships within it."

CHUCK COWAN
OPINION RESEARCHER
Washington, D.C.

WHAT I DO:
I'm both chief statistician and vice president for advanced analytical methods at an opinion research firm. We're a company that helps other businesses find better ways to market their products. To do this, we gather and then analyze data about people's behavior.

I have two distinct functions. As chief statistician, I oversee the quality of our studies, and I also help researchers with statistical or other math problems. For example, a researcher might know a lot about a specific issue such as the environment, but not a lot about the mathematics involved in researching opinions about it. I don't know about the issue, but I do understand how to research it. I know how to focus on a body of data and find the hidden relationships within it.

One of our studies is for the postal service. We measure customer satisfaction on a quarterly basis, and suggest ways to improve performance. When we find a change in customer satisfaction, we try to determine whether it was caused by a change in postal service operations, or by some outside factor. I design sampling procedures, so that we know which people it would be helpful to survey. I also review the questions being asked, in order to create a few summary measures that describe satisfaction in general.

As vice president of advanced analytical methods, I sell my mathematical expertise to outside groups that have their own data. For example, I did some work for an automobile manufacturer.

Chuck examines data from an opinion survey commissioned by one of his clients.

This study measures satisfaction with the postal service.

I looked at a year's worth of records, checking cars bought in six different countries. I did this to determine which cars were in direct competition with each other.

HOW I GOT STARTED:
I first heard of statistics in my senior year of college. Until then, I'd been studying English. But I knew that it would be hard to get a job in that field, so I had a double major in English and economics. As a requirement for the economics degree, I was forced to take a course in statistics. That was how I became familiar with the subject. Eventually, I went on to get a master's in economet-

rics, which is the study of the mathematics used in measuring the economy. I also got a doctorate in mathematical statistics.

HOW I FEEL ABOUT IT:
This work is very creative. There are many different ways to sample a group or analyze a set of data, but my job is to find the best way. It's a math problem, but on a very large scale. Once you get good at math, though, you have all sorts of tools that you can use to solve problems.

One problem is that clients are very issue-oriented but don't have much technical background. It's sometimes difficult to explain the results to them, even though they're interested, because they don't have the technical background to understand what you're telling them. In this respect, I think my English background has contributed a lot to my success.

WHAT YOU SHOULD KNOW: It's important to be well-rounded. To do this job, you need to know the math, and you have to pay attention to the details. But you also need to be able to communicate. You're dealing with people and their needs, and you have to be able to understand those needs in order to meet them.

You can get into this field with a B.A. in math or statistics, but it's a good idea to get an advanced degree. The more training you have, the more tools you'll have to work with.

The pay is good, as it is in most math-related fields. Entry-level people start in the range of $30,000 per year, and most people peak at between $60,000 and $70,000. Some people with expertise in special areas, though, make a great deal more than that.

Computer-generated graphs help interpret raw data.

"I realized right away that there was a lot of diversity in the work."

BRUCE JONES

ACTUARY

Piscataway, New Jersey

WHAT I DO:
I work for a life insurance company. We have four basic products: life insurance, health insurance, pension plans, and annuities. I work in the pension area. I'm responsible for pricing our pension products.

One of the more difficult things to explain about what I do is the idea that pension plans, or insurance policies in general, are products that must be priced. People understand how manufacturing products are priced. There's the cost of labor, materials, and overhead, plus profit. But when you're talking about the price of a pension plan, you're talking about the premium that the insurance company has to charge in order to cover expected costs.

We set premiums using

math almost exclusively. To set the premium rate for a pension plan, we have to calculate when people can be expected to retire and what benefits they will likely receive. The premium has to be set so that the plan will generate enough money to cover the anticipated benefits.

Pension plan rate-setting includes a lot of interest rate calculations, as well as assumptions about the beneficiary's lifespan. With health and life insurance policies, however, the mathematics of probability is just as important. Because life insurance policies pay out death benefits, it's very important when setting premium rates to know the chances of each policy holder dying. If there's a high probability of mortality, then the premium will have to be high. If it's low, the premium can be low. It's an actuary's job to study statistical information and make these determinations.

HOW I GOT STARTED:

I always did well in math. In fact, when I got to college, I majored in math and decided that I wanted to be a high school math teacher. But when I started doing student teaching back in the late 1970s, I found teaching to be very frustrating. The pay was low and a lot of teachers were looking for other jobs. So I decided to look at other things. I had a friend who was an actuary, and he convinced me to consider the field.

HOW I FEEL ABOUT IT:

Right from the start, I liked this field. I realized right away that there was a lot of diversity in the work. Also, I'd always been interested in continuing my education, and this job gave me an opportunity to do that. When you're an actuary, you take a series of qualifying exams to become certified. These exams test your proficiency at the skills required to be an actuary. My employer gave me study time so I could study to pass them.

One discouraging aspect of the work is the public's perception of the field. A recent study rated actuarial work as number one in job satisfaction, but most discussions of the field tend to be negative. Actuaries are viewed as stodgy, boring people who work off in a

Bruce helps a colleague study for the qualifying exams.

Actuaries use calculations to determine premium rates.

room somewhere, doing calculations. But that's just not the case.

WHAT YOU SHOULD KNOW:
One thing I want to stress is that there's a lot of diversity both in the job and in the field. Actuaries work in many different settings — universities, consulting firms, life insurance companies, and the government, to name a few. So there's something for everyone who has the interest and the aptitude.

If you're interested in actuarial work, it's best to start by getting a good liberal arts background in college. Take math, business, and accounting courses. Then, once you've taken enough math, take the preliminary actuarial exam and see how you feel about it. Also, look up the local actuarial club. Every major metropolitan area has one. These clubs can provide you with additional information, as well as put you in touch with people in the field who can give you the benefits of their own experience.

The hours and the pay are comparable to those in other professions such as the law and certified public accounting. In my experience, the hours have been cyclical. There are slow times, and then there are very busy times when I'm working long hours and even weekends.

"I have the opportunity to spark an interest that might otherwise not develop."

JOEL SCHNEIDER

MATH TV CONTENT DIRECTOR

New York, New York

WHAT I DO:
I'm the content director for "Square One TV," which is a half-hour television show about mathematics. Part of my job is to make sure that the math on each show is correct and that it's at the right level for our audience. Our target audience is eight- to twelve-year-olds, but our actual audience is much broader than that. I also propose concepts and ideas for future shows.

In the early stages of program development, for example, a writer, lyricist, or animator might be looking for a mathematical problem to write a piece or a song about. Or one of them might already have an idea into which math has to be fit. My staff and I give them sugges- tions as to what will work.

Later, when the show is actually in production, we worry about props and set design because both have mathematical components that need to be reviewed. We may need a particular prop, like a pie to illustrate a circle graph or a map for a sketch on ratios.

I also help to make sure that everything on the show reinforces the math. For example, I watch to see that the camera angles show what needs to be shown, and that actors deliver certain lines as written if the lines are essential to the piece's math content.

HOW I GOT STARTED:
In junior high school, a key event turned me toward the idea of mathematics as a career. Until then, math was just one of my many in- terests. But when I was in the eighth grade, I read a novel that involved a geomet-

Joel selects props to be used on the program.

ric construction. Because I was curious about what that construction would look like, I asked a teacher, and the teacher said just the right thing: "Why don't you see if you can figure it out yourself?"

Although at that time the math was beyond my capabilities, I worked on the problem for a few years, on and off. The work I did on that problem was so significant to me that it got me thinking about being a mathemetician.

I studied math in college and went on to get both a master's degree and a doctorate. Then I got a job at Penn State University. I also designed math courses for students who were studying to be elementary school teachers. That's when I became interested in math education.

HOW I FEEL ABOUT IT:
There are three basic things that I like about this work. The first is that there's tremendous variety. I work with a lot of talented people who are creative in many different ways and fields. Related to that is the fact that everything I've ever been interested in — music, math, language — is useful in this work. And the third thing I like about my work is that the job gives me the opportunity to do something useful. I have the opportunity to give kids a positive experience with math and to spark an interest that might otherwise

not develop. We have a daily audience of a million people. That gives our show the potential to have a great impact.

WHAT YOU SHOULD KNOW: Basically, there are several different ways to get into educational television work. You can come to it as I have, through expertise in a subject area. Or you can get involved with television production work. You can also approach it through the creative end — writing, acting, or doing animation.

There are a few prerequisites, though, for my particular job. One is a specialty in mathematics. Beyond that, you have to have a willing-ness to deal with people who are outside the field of mathematics. It goes without saying that you have to be able to communicate very well or no one will under-stand you, including the audience.

The pay is good. Someone in my position — a content director with a doctorate — can command a salary that's comparable to, or slightly higher than, the salaries at big universities. The hours, however, can be tough. We don't punch a time clock or get summers off. We work until the program is done, and that can mean 10- and 12-hour days, and even weekend work.

"Square one TV" uses many approaches to teach math.

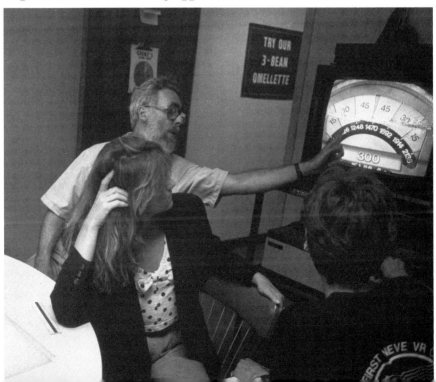

"I like the camaraderie of the navy and the feeling that I'm doing a job that's necessary."

CMDR. JAMES TERRY THORNTON

U.S. NAVY OFFICER

Washington, D.C.

WHAT I DO:
I've been in the navy for 18 years, and in that time I've held many different jobs. Earlier in my career, I served on several different ships. Through these assignments and further training, I acquired an excellent background in the technical side of advanced weapons systems. Later, I studied management, and that prepared me for the job I have now: military resources management director.

My first assignment after I was commissioned into the navy in 1971 was as an anti-submarine warfare officer aboard a 1940s-era destroyer. Soon I moved up to a more modern destroyer, and then finally to a state-of-the-art guided-missile destroyer. While these ships varied in

James's career has included service on a destroyer as an anti-submarine officer.

the state of their technology and in the systems they carried, all three jobs required a strong grounding in mathematics. A knowledge of statistics is particularly important because as an anti-sub officer you're constantly dealing with probabilities, such as the probability that an enemy sub is in one place and not another.

The job also requires an understanding of physics. Take sonar, for instance. Sonar is like underwater radar. It sends and receives pulses of sound that can help locate objects underwater, objects like submarines. To understand sonar, however, and to be able to interpret what the machines tell you, you've got to understand the physics of both sound and water.

Now that I no longer serve on a ship, I have less use for my sonar skills. I'm still involved with math, but it's management math now. After a series of different assignments, I went to naval post-graduate school in 1981, where I got a master's in management science that prepared me to be an analyst in the fields of manpower, personnel, and training.

Now, among other responsibilities, I handle personnel management for equipment procurement programs. Systems Command will come to me with a request for personnel to run procurement programs, such as for satellite systems or radars, and my job is to review those requests for technical accuracy. If a request is approved, I help fill the position.

HOW I GOT STARTED:
My father was in the air force for 27 years, so I grew up around the military, and that predisposed me toward a military career. Because the prospect of travel appealed to me, I chose the navy. I went to college on a navy ROTC scholarship. ROTC stands for Reserve Officer Training Corps.

HOW I FEEL ABOUT IT:
In general, I like the camaraderie of the navy and the feeling that I'm doing a

James is an expert in sonar and radar technology.

James demonstrates the skills of an anti-sub officer.

ing places, doing exciting things. But travel can also have its down side. You don't have time to build roots, and, more importantly, there's a lot of family separation involved. For example, in 1976, I was away from the United States for all but six weeks. My daughter was born that year, and I didn't get to see her until she was five months old.

WHAT YOU SHOULD KNOW: The navy is becoming an increasingly technical organization. The new ships and planes coming on line are all state-of-the-art, so an individual coming into the navy now has to have a good grounding in both math and science. Also, whether you're an enlisted person fixing a piece of sophisticated equipment or an officer in a management or leadership position, you're required to do a lot of reading and assimilating of information. So you need to have good language skills as well.

job that's necessary. From my perspective, the world's not always a safe place, and while I'm not anxious to go to war, I do recognize the need for a strong defensive capability. It gives me a sense of satisfaction to do something that I think is important.

Another thing that I've liked about the navy has been the travel — seeing interest-

Navy salaries depend on the job. Besides base pay, there are special situations, such as flight pay for pilots or nuclear pay for submarine personnel. But to give you an idea, navy officers make approximately $20,000 to $75,000 a year in pay and allowances, while enlisted personnel earn between $10,000 and $35,000.

"Understanding the math involved in gaming gives you an edge."

DON CROCKET
CASINO MANAGER

Reno, Nevada

WHAT I DO:

As vice president of casino management for Bally's Reno Casino, I oversee all of the gaming activity in the complex. That includes the slot machines, keno, and all of the table games: craps, 21, roulette, baccarat, and poker.

One of my main concerns is the casino's profit level, and obviously there's a lot of math involved with that, mostly statistics. For each game, for example, I keep track of what we win and what we lose on a daily basis. Then I use this information to calculate something called the hold percentage. The hold percentage is the ratio of the money the casino keeps to the total amount of money that players put into slots or spend on chips.

Don looks over the day's casino records. He uses them to calculate the hold percentage for each game.

To attract more business, we use advertising and promotion, but sometimes we'll also implement new rules more favorable to the customer. In considering any of these options, we always weigh the costs and the benefits. We use statistics to calculate whether or not the cost of each new option will be more than offset by the expected increase in business.

HOW I GOT STARTED:

I was around casinos from an early age. As a kid, I spent most of my summers in Lake Tahoe, where there are a lot of them. Later, dealing was a summer job that helped me work my way through college.

HOW I FEEL ABOUT IT:

I like the variation in this job. I deal with lots of different people — players and employees — and I get to see them interacting in an exciting environment. A casino is

Don and a co-worker discuss operation of the casino.

always interesting, and you're never quite sure what you're going to see.

WHAT YOU SHOULD KNOW:
Experience as a dealer is almost mandatory for someone in my position. You can do some casino management jobs — in marketing or finance — without dealing experience. But to do my job, which is running the games, you have to know them from the floor level.

Understanding the math involved in gaming also gives you an edge. In roulette, for example, there are 38 possible numbers that can come up. This means that over the course of many, many spins of the wheel, the casino should win 37 out of every 38 individual number bets. If the table profits show something else, then it's time to take a closer look.

The pay in casinos is very good. A good dealer can make $30,000 in the first year, including tips. Experienced dealers at top casinos have made well over $100,000 in a single year. But the pay can be a trap. It's so good that people sometimes resist moving on, even if they're tired of dealing.

The management job immediately above dealing pays a salary that is often less than what a dealer can make with tips. But for a smart dealer who's interested, there's lots of room for advancement, and the top levels of management can be quite lucrative.

Related Careers

Here are more math-related careers
you may want to explore:

AEROSPACE ENGINEER
Aerospace engineers design,
develop, and test airplanes, missiles,
and spacecraft.

BOOKKEEPER
Bookkeepers maintain the financial
records of businesses and are often
responsible for payroll and banking
as well.

BIOMEDICAL ENGINEER
Biomedical engineers use
engineering techniques to solve
health-related problems. They
design such devices as artificial
limbs and pacemakers for the heart.

**CERTIFIED PUBLIC
ACCOUNTANT (CPA)**
Certified public accountants are
hired by businesses and individuals
to prepare tax returns, business
plans, and financial reports.

ECONOMIST
Economists study the way people do
business to determine how society's
resources can be most effectively
managed.

ELECTRICAL ENGINEER
Electrical engineers design
electronic equipment such as
stereos, computers, and radar.

INSURANCE UNDERWRITER
Underwriters analyze the financial
risks involved in issuing insurance
policies and then decide whether or
not to issue them.

MATHEMATICAL TECHNICIAN
Mathematical technicians are
specialists in math who work with
research scientists to help them
solve technological problems.

METEOROLOGIST
Meteorologists study the earth's
atmosphere. The most common
application of their work is weather
forecasting, but meteorologists also
work with air pollution control and
fire prevention.

PURCHASING AGENT
Purchasing agents buy — at the
lowest possible cost — the supplies,
materials, and equipment needed
for a company to do business.

ROBOTICS ENGINEER
Robotics engineers design
computer-controlled machines, or
robots, that are used in factories to
perform repetitive tasks.

**THEORETICAL
MATHEMATICIAN**
Theoretical mathematicians work
with existing mathematical
knowledge to develop new theories
and principles.

You may also want to investigate
the growing number of computer-
related careers, which also use
math skills.

Organizations

Contact these organizations for information
about the following careers:

PHYSICIST
American Association of Physics Teachers
5112 Berwyn Road, College Park, MD 20740

SURVEYOR
American Congress on Surveying and Mapping
5410 Grosvenor Lane, Suite 100, Bethesda, MD 20814

ACCOUNTANT
American Institute of C.P.A.'s, Division of Relations with Educators
1121 Sixth Avenue, New York, NY 10036

GENERAL MATHEMATICS
Association for Women in Mathematics, P.O. Box 178, Wellesley, MA 02181

STATISTICIAN
Center for Statistical Sciences
University of Texas at Austin, Mathematics Department, Austin, TX 78712

ACCOUNTANT
Financial Analyst Federation, P.O. Box 3668, Charlottesville, VA 22903

MATHEMATICS AND PHYSICS
International Association of Mathematical Physics
Department of Mathematics, University of Florida
201 Walker Street, Gainesville, FL 32611

NAVY OFFICER
Navy Opportunity Information Center
P.O. Box 9406, Gaithersburg, MD 20898

GEOPHYSICIST, GEOLOGIST, SEISMOLOGIST
Seismographic Stations, University of California, Berkeley
Department of Geology and Geophysics, Berkeley, CA 94720

ACTUARY
Society of Actuaries, 475 N. Martingale Road, Schaumburg, IL 60173

APPLIED MATHEMATICS
Society for Industrial and Applied Mathematics
Science Center, 3600 University City, Philadelphia, PA 19104-2688

ROBOTICS
Society of Manufacturing Engineers
Attn: Manager of Manufacturing Engineers Education
1 S.M.E. Drive, Dearborn, MI 48121

ENGINEERING
Society for Women Engineers
345 East 47 Street, Room 305, New York, NY 10017

Books

CAREER CHOICES FOR STUDENTS OF ECONOMICS
By Career Associates. New York: Walker & Co., 1985.

CAREER CHOICES FOR STUDENTS OF MATHEMATICS
By Career Associates. New York: Walker & Co., 1985.

CAREER OPPORTUNITIES IN GEOLOGY AND THE EARTH SCIENCES
By Lisa A. Rossbacher. New York: Arco Publishing, 1983.

CAREER TRACKS
By Lester Schwartz and Irv Brechuer. New York: Ballantine Books, 1985.

CAREERS IN ACCOUNTING
By G. Gaylord and G. Ried. Homewood, Ill.: Dow Jones-Irwin, 1984.

CAREERS IN SCIENCE
By Thomas A. Easton. Chicago: National Textbook Co., 1984.

THE COMPLETE GUIDE TO ENVIRONMENTAL CAREERS
By the CEIP Fund. Washington, D.C.: Island Press, 1989.

JOBS FOR THE 21ST CENTURY
By Robert V. Weinstein. New York: Collier Books, 1983.

ADVICE TO A YOUNG SCIENTIST
By P. B. Medawar. New York: Harper & Row, 1979.

140 HIGH-TECH CAREERS
By Bob Weinstein. New York: Collier Books, 1985.

OPPORTUNITIES IN FINANCIAL CAREERS
By Michael Sunichrast and Dean Crist. Chicago: National Textbook Co., 1985.

PETERSON'S ENGINEERING, SCIENCE AND COMPUTER JOBS, 11th Edition
Amy J. Goldstein, Editor. Princeton, N.J.: Peterson's Guides, 1990.

SPACE CAREERS
By C. Sheffield and C. Rosin. New York: William Morrow, 1983.

SUCCESS GUIDE FOR ACCOUNTANTS
By Robert Haef. New York: McGraw-Hill, 1984.

YOUR CAREER IN ENGINEERING
By William F. Shanahan. New York: Arco Publishing, 1981.

Glossary Index